AF529440

Rhapsody

INSIGHT PUBLICA

Nadakkavu, Kozhikode, Kerala, 673011
www.insightpublica.com
e-mail: insightpublica@gmail.com
Title: **Rhapsody**
(Poems in English)
Author: **Anjali A. Nair**
Cover Design: kjvj
First Edition: March 2022

Printed and Published by
InsightinPublica Printers & Publishers Pvt. Ltd.
ISBN 978-93-5517-049-1

RHAPSODY

Poems in English

Anjali A. Nair

INSIGHT PUBLICA®

DEDICATED TO

THE LOTUS FEET OF BHAGAWAN

SRI SATHYA SAI BABA

Anjali.A. Nair studied in St.Joseph's Anglo - Indian School, Calicut. She took her Bachelors and Masters in English Lit. From Providence Womens College, Calicut and Calicut University respectively, getting a high first class at both levels. Later she took her BEd in English from Calicut Training College. She is fond of writing, specially verses. Her devotion to Sri Sathya Sai Baba is complete.

She is staying with her parents at Saileela, Sadanam Road, Calicut. Mob: 9447174385

She has published 6 books including the present

ANJALI.A.NAIR

ACKNOWLEDGEMENT

I am much obliged to the inner resident, the voice of God, my conscience which speaks to me,who is Sai Bhagawan, really who prompts my activities, where by this book has been brought about. My parents, l adore, in their company my numb brain gets creative. My father, Mr Achuthan Nair and mother, Prof , Smt Bharathi A. Nair, hugs to you by way of thanks. My brother, Mr Dinesh. A. Nair, Project Engineer, Fujiara, his wife, Meera, son, Achuthan give me smiles of encouragement. I thank, sincerely Smt Rekha Sati Raveendran for her Computer services. I acknowledge Insight Publication, who kindly published the work .

Pranam

Prayer

A LISP UNTO THINE EAR

O! Sai Krishna!
you are the cynosure of all eyes,
the song in the ear
I long to feed thee, with sweetness like sugar,
that a herdess may tread on her anklet,
weaving garlands with which to embrace you with my own arms
my tone to melt thy mood
to enjoy the benefit of thy company,
O! Lord, the cynosure of all eyes
do not destroy my devotion
thy essence being like honey
I adore, oh! only too much,
there is gladness in my inner being
which ,dispels the darkness of sadness
I again, over- whelm thee with passion
for pure, new adventures
what you have always given is always heaven,
of all these realms, you are the sovereign
the pangs of the memories of separation bring much pain
but I am going to forget these
only, so that you may continue your dance, un-inhibited.

Preface

Naivette, that l am.

I am fighting some degrees of naivette. I seem unable to understand the world. Formerly, I had been very abashed and shy but with a beautifully lit conscience and surrounded by my family, my kith and kin I liked. My naiveness was very acceptable to Bhagawan Sri Sathya Sai Baba, who could see I was but a simpleton. I became naiver at His attention and the world soon became secondary. I was given to tantrums but mostly my wishes were all full- filled. Nobody would call me naivette but I find it all too difficult to adjust to this world. What divine gifts that had been in me seem to have evaporated and now they are all too assimilated in my system .I had strong resistance which came from love for God. Chanting of His name makes me meritorious, with caution because I had been holding it , dear, I regard I am a spiritual whirl - pool . Wherefore can I.... pavements? be cleansed to walk the road, nay, the pavements. My fears are all about being snuffed out for I know naught what keeps brewing only that it may be in the Divine will be something good, for my betterment. I am aghast at fighting this naiveness of belonging to the world but I realise now after such a criteria that we passed through that I am not the lone person and that the same God is with me assuring.

INDEX

A NOTE ON BENEVOLENCE

Indeed love were better be expressed thro' timely blossoms
that it caters to the dreams
and counter- visions of us mani-fold
hidden acute within, it lays barren
making a waste-land of the grounds of another
by chance made capital, if it fructify!
most amazing are the sprouts that germinate
it doth provide soulful nourishment to a stranger
satiating the pangs of hunger
thus be the love of a person, silent and with-drawn
meant finally for the benevolence of all.

ABUNDANT LIKE WINE

A shallow pond that does not lillies flounder
like the barren trough with no hope
whatsoever of greenery
still the lake, lengthless whose waters are waded
for the safety of it's shore ,
inanimicable be thy pledge,
that hours passing does bring near to the shrunk,
abundant wine in goblets ,measures and measures
filled with heady sensations.

SOJOURN

Nor do we want that it should go on and on
as mountains grow steeper
and harder to climb
the oceans assuming depth ere we troop to fall
the sky, then to suit our fancy
sharp comes the realization
that we have no further to trek
but only to lay ourselves down
some place comfortable,
to obtain where there are no thorns to prick
that alone being our quest.

OF LANDS, NOWHERE

We dream of stuff that are not to be
a slice of cake, with icing is what life is meant,
can we dream of wine berry mountains to land in?
no, that pudding cart is not our dwelling!
we but melt the ice-cream and assimilate on our tongue, it's wholesomeness,
snow-peaks not being our habitation
we but dream, just like that
what, we cannot make our own
that defining, of
suffocation of life
caught by it's tirade fanciful
outdone by it's demands, protocol
is, is, oh! so overwhelming! .

GO! GAIN IT

Dreaming doth make it splendrous
the half - truth being the numbness, we recoil from
dis-enchantment of worldly gains brings it brings about
times are when they keep forgetting the strain betwixt their labour
reflecting upon it yonder maketh us tick
with eccelectic elan,
human sport is love - we fancy,
it's what is to be pondered!
beyond, outta reach,
some day , yet to be within the grasp, the grasp of all, all, the yearning;
this tabernacle of heavenly treacle
fills our gut maleficently.....
our purpose is targetted.

PINKY MISTS

The infinite sky, looking,
I gain depths
it 's outpouring sonnet
failing to retrieve!....
some day I must clear those pinky mists
then on to flow as a lake
with girdles that make it prance
my eyes are moist and harden like dew
because I never believed it would ever be
then I smile at all the disturbance
because they sourly crack my many sins.

SEEK THOU, THE EVER- LASTING

The present with it's simmering hope of
payasams that are delectable ,
hurriedly vanishes, as well too
like the change of guards who are on duty,
old values are exchanged by modern mannerisms speaking tall
ah! the ever- lasting is always never ending
what seemingly pleases tho'
by it's reverberation of refrains
is the blinking eye of the living entirety
wherein all creatures smile,
united as in one chord,
are those pleasantries meaning something
that it establishes inner accord which ensemble
what we know as the Supreme poise.

WHAT FOR?

Care- worn days approach
restlessness be by-gone
tomorrow, most unlikely a peer
the present, an ice- berg ,
which with its canine teeth is devouring !
my pleasures are disappearing
indulgence shy away
age sets soon to be rooted-
I glimpse a chamber of promise
which entering upon ascertained consel
I shall imperiously recover
finding my longed for placements.

MASKS

Nor do I encapsulate
a future for me
that is full of bright buttons of hope
I see days of restricted leisure,
of freedom that barks unwelcome, -
for l lie as in cradle
where on l gaze upon the sky
smiling at the beaming face of the moon
the dazzling sheet of sunlight,
I find cozier
than all of the attention of the world
what gives me the utmost joy is but
frisking into papa 's lauding arms
and always jubilant at mama's wise words of wisdom
I've never been out of the cradle
I prefer being bolted in.

GREAT, GREATER IS THY POMP

There be less glamour in my home
than there be in all the regions pervading
there be more vital essence in the vast orbits
beyond the two hemispheres of the earth
there be pomp superseding in the space
outer these orbits distancing
and beyond there be the stars multi-hued studded
where in his lordliness,Sri Sathya Sai Bhagawan is reclining,
attentive to the resonant prayers emanating
from the persuasive lips as well too of filling the
flask full with delicious malt and chocolate to all the needy.

OF SUPER- FINE THOUGHTS

This vagabond that paces unfamiliar tertia,
is the mind,
I trust not it's whereabouts
rather I favour the ripples
that enchant by its lithe onrush of
super-fine thoughts
which swings in the periggrine lake
and harbours the maddonic sentiments man is made of.

THE GOAL

Perceiving that a new era would dawn golden and fair
that the race of man are all regarded same as one
dream on and on the Oracle proclaimed,
the summation is much attractive
reproach not the future!
a millennium of temptations does not heroes distract
who always walks in front
is near to God,
being dear
he moves fastest with elan to the goal which him doth beguile.

NO BAD REELS

To think big is to grow bigger
that never a calamity doth befall
somebody with a mantle brave
evil, determinedly not over-reach
woh! there be no depression
but scintillating life
that rolls on and on
like waves of the ocean
caught a rye, a whiff; -
broad surf's
to where no bad reels.

REPRIEVE

Of late am l grown bashful,
the song of the summer upon my ear
whistling notes be,
that pronounce a past of meaningness full
I'd been longing reprieve,
set at naught
blinks at creation and it's undulating expressiveness of charm
thus am I contained as of today
reconnaissant about the wonders,
what times of the future ought to spring.

THE ELIXER

A specimen of sorts
that writhe in agony
nigh impossible to wrest free of the commotion life causeth
nothing is by accident nor mere chance goes un- noticed
deigned by God is the gaga-
He alone taketh it away
the swoon of after- life is much in his hands
the good are indeed lucky
the one's struggling too perchance taste the elixer.

VIBRANT

By my own innocence am I throttled
ever the vibrant
new life speaks on
much like the sprouts
forgets soon it's sorrow as an embryo
prolonged is the over-rule
of the laws of creation
of life permeating,
of the waxing and waning of the moon, like-wise of joy and sorrow,
of the mixing and separating of ties.

THAT OF A TYPHOON

The cannibal remained incognito
leaping always with the shadow
slapping the conscience- stricken
all who would never move
t' were like an avalanche striking
the imbalance steamed,
soon became an hurricane
aversion was popular,
as for dear live 's sake all the good men and women
conselled , the cannibal was ensnared,
aflared , he became terror- riding, wailed, moaned and
erupted into a creeping typhoon,
invisible,
tottering the multitudes.

DEAR DEW DROPS...

Drops of dew signify the morning lullness
they drench the flora and fauna
giving them their chillness
dew drops from plants also trickle on to the human frames,
horripulating
they swallow the day's heat,
awakens man to the dreary as well too to the drab monotony.

ODE TO SLUMBER

I did suddenly fall asleep
shutting away that is not mine
waves of peace, refreshful doled
I gave myself to slumber uncaring
a lot of passionate longings nestled
all over my pores as in a trough
then many diwas were lit
I sailed a voyage, unpredicted as in a lore.....
lastly, I woke up coming to Thee,
craving for thy mercy, again to be

A LULLABY

The brink from which I perspire
seeing naught tomorrow
invisible as hope
lullabies that intone
fanning glad hearts
evinces a supposition,
we have each other and we are all
infallible though dauntless
the sparkle always leading
fumbling nor fidgety
always in His trail,
ah! intractable but He is with us.

OF CAPES ABOVE

I wish to hop on to the clouds
and wend a way to regions across
where my future lies
where alone I see hope shimmering bright
my furore sped
I shall wake up to a harmless blizzard
no more daring but adventurous
I shall sing a nice lullaby
to rock my dear one's asleep
I will only then be feigning anger
but the storm shall pass smooth
the love I will then star- mouth
will be full as I ever imagined it would be
I will also sear afloat
in the abundant capes
being close to all I hold dear
thus I shall overcome fear and be set at last free.

ECHOES

We are not vile by purpose
bestial temptations monger
we know of ourselves as a dudgeon
wilderness, soon gone
bland as well preoccupied
stubborn as ox the frail
fickle our thoughts with crookedness swaying,
but the palms of areca-nut and kera mumble strong, their rustling fawning,
like fields that are solicitously irrigated....
but here is the spark of the living,
responsive to love and all those echoes,
looming! which has wide open arms, the warmth- which to lighten ! .

LOST

When in oblivion and quite lost, it was then , God, alone who came to me,
He held my hand....
I gained something .
the spasms of breath resumed quick
very soon, I anticipated a fragrance....
which inhaling I headed back
to the plateaus of the juvenile earth.

OF MY OWN

I put the strength all of a bull
into an apparition
at heart I am timid, faint, keep pausing
at every erroneous blunder ,
I trembled,
to make a marvel of my own
I wish, my monstrous labour of creation would win
and I continue to overreach,
enjoying my fall and spring,
then, receding quite, quite forgetful of time ,
I grow fretful and wary of strangers who plausibly keep intrud-
ing.

IN AGONY

Fantasies, that are remain splintered
not a single hope to cling to any bosom,
strange, the air to breathe
the tracks, yet tarry to tread
seemingly living in gooseberry land with notable sentiments
that warm
a unpredicted drizzle no more doth bring the smile upon a face
alas! no more doth the blush hover upon the lips,
can we, volp a starry tomorrow
with the romantic past shrunk
leaving the present only eagerness and worries of agonized
deliberations.

LET ME NOT, THEE, NEGLECT

I don't know what will make me turn toward the earth , accept its realness and falsity,
it's harshness and thrashing nightmare of ill- fateful consequences
embroiled by each circumstance
am I blinded having travelled
far and searching spaces
and there is in the pores of my eyes
which
only camphor may soothe
alas! running away brought me infinite harm!
I remember only the mess as how I came upon the world and it derided,
there be very , many forbidden lands l strain to encroach
somehow I belong nowhere but everywhere is there within my reach-
Oh! mother, venerable earth! ,
Let me not, Thee, neglect.

OF REFORMATION

A moment of rue
obsessions with the fabulous
temperamental to success
desultory climate
demeaning mannerisms
make on a bold move
start undoing your harm.

O! EARTH! SMILE

We of the earth love it ‘s warmth and coziness,
it ‘s dexterous arms which are trees
it ‘s vast expanses of water that lash us clean
it ‘s plushy comfort which are tall grasses pruned
it ‘s mountains which are marble breasts
the mud baked huts that be lush as humble,
where we are to laugh some time together
transported, thereafter to frurore destinations.

ON THIS TERRA-COTTA

It may come about sooner than we always hoped
or, it may take a long, long time-
our tenure on this terra-cotta speedily
heading toward termination,
is bothersome
such a nuisance
are we relaxed? at leisure?,
we can but sigh
at the pleasures afforded
because they are all so pain- stakingly wrought
we cannot have liberation bottled our days are never meant to
be extended
nor does release come about pre- mature
we, we must always enjoin upon ourselves
that future days to come will be very, very sweet.

THAT I WAS

I laugh like the sea
I breathe like the sun-flower
live in ghastly and ghostly surroundings
irked at the past having gone
unwelcoming the present
drawn to a future, stringent,
I will be a dame moulded sparingly
I see the harshness writ all over
I faintly recede,
I am no more the bud, poignant
that I was.

RECAPITULATION

As it were dangerous illness which we bear
will not be too prolonged too
solicitiousness does it shield and
guard nicely
suddenly vanishes into thin air
the whereabouts of which, we know hardly
are perturbed, the vast concourse of generations that passed on
we just conjecture
into far better climate and atmosphere reproved
there where our prattle assume
meaninglessness of the strangling we left behind.

OF COW- HERDS AND THE LORD

Always say to yourself,
I am beautiful
alike the figurines of frolicsome herds and herdessess
I am of the stature of the highest auspiciousness
pleasantries and misfortune become me
my coming upon the world was an incidental phenomenon,
a divine supposition
I am aware of that God resides in my heart
and always works for my benefit
dark shadows that linger are never meant for all time
my chance is championed already, for I have called out to Him
nay, I am but puppet with elastic strings that cling on to His
body
ah! from the primeval times
where then!, should I the excellence seek!?,
but in me!,
I am extra-ordinary, that is the truth.

DAWN

I am falling for the world, Lord
before I sink into it's quagmire
let my eyes seep some joy
at thy behest
persisting long enough
for the suffocation to cease and not to retain lure for it's lustre, I
mis- construe
in the hassle- tassle of daylight
as in the wrenching times, Lord,
I am bound by these pythons to be led astray
so let me search for thy nectarine sweetness
at least for small minutes now
which like dew
most, certainly waft my eye-lids
the day- time long.

MAROONED

If only I could forget that I am not the only person
marooned in an isle
that the world that comes in between
is to make me smile
its pathetic but I can't yell as usual I do,
consolably,God seems to hear my cry
though I 've turned mute
I appeal to you to forgive me because I am in appearance deaf
to your plea
it's only that I am alive to a situation
which I trust is good to me
I am not against to your gossip
but I tremble
because it cannot set
me hovering toward my destiny I
prefer
so let me shake your hand and bid good-bye
seeking refuge inside the doors of
this super-fluous vistage which is of occupation mine.

KEEPS DANCING

Where does all my wondering go?!,
at the lapse of elation am I zero
the pantomime of my demonstration keeps dancing
my heart beat is racing
is shy of all those whiteness
no more intimidate!,
I am shorn of illusion
full of glee in the day- light
with a small longing for thy caressing touch ever soft like petals.

SPEAK ON, LIFE

Child- hood , one of the sweetness of pudding
adolescence, screeching alike the midget
woman- hood, regal et elite' and brusque
middle age, hath convictions rigid
old age, with nephra- worldly addictions
the life of man, is thus tampered with.

LIKE A SHREW

Wantonly doth infuriation make it a shrew
of tempests, we hardly know that blow uneasy,
upsetting,
it doth take the time to restore decorum,
to smoothen the edge,
letting calmness, slowly descend.

THE UNCHANGED

The vigorous dial of day casts hard a bearing
loathe as ever the newer cleave and dexterous clouds that torment while passing,
in time that's never meant to stand still
I am as ever unchanged, placid and well.

SWAMI AND DARSHAN

Days be bygone when Sai Maharaj reigned
days that were crusted, delectable like almond, raisin,
cashew and pistachio
filled with ultra- worldly detail of movements and sensations
those days galore!,
where sins were immediately burnt to ashes
joy, incredible prevailed and peace, submission , love
memories, still, sentiments treasured
never to retreat
from the cones of our hearts
where they barge handsomely
making a millionaire of those, thus be-set.
40. Splendora
The days spun
I heeded them not
always hidden as a calf
but not certain of my own identity
I was shovelled as a plum
relievingly not to be savoured
alas! I kept away,
running away for miles to be understanding me,
once, I realise my preciousness
days of splendora are definitely drawing near.

MY PLAY-HOUSE

What greatness issue forth from the earnest depths being your deliberate plan
because I feel incompetent,
the sand- castles that I built upon the shores of the beach
are my play-house
fairly, not to be raided!,
yet, alas! , I am no different
from the common race
because I am also falling, falling to the atrocities of the surviving taciturn.

IN THYSELF

Deeply enmeshed as I am in thine own being
not knowing of whence headed
the walls of the Universe within which I am entrapped , hold
minute promise
for l am as a dove in a cage
loved for her ludicrous charm ! ,
thus to behold !,
for l am one of those
who craved for thy attentive comradeship ,
that , being my avowed destiny.

A NEW HAVEN

I want badly to strander to some place
which I designate is pleasant enough
to breathe the air sweet
I think nobody will mind it here
that l scowl or scream
the bad will all go flying
my eyes may drip with snow
I will lie in my father's lap and smile at my mother and family
forgetful and rested
replenished in a new haven
where alone it is so peaceful.

SLOWLY, WE REALISE

We but belong here, verily here itself
our joys are meaningfully apportioned
sorrows never too tumultuous
ere they be borne meticulously
by other kindred
fatigue, affliction, distaste
soon doth pass
ah! we are to remain silent, whilst, prosperity is ushered surreptitiously
at chance, or by intervals
life being a fe'te that disappears on the legitimate shores of the eaves of Sai, the Almighty God;
slowly, we realise we are His same Swaroopa.

AWAKENING

The instant joy rages simultaneously
trouble- shooting memorabilia vanishes
we be bourne light
stopping only on enquiry within,
what is this?, I have forgotten
it is only meaningless sorrow
genuinely shouldered by huge and mighty arms truly apprehended as belonging to God
the sprays of which rays of the moon sporting wide a smile,
courage and conviction infuse
where by malady is done with and we awaken unto ourselves of which is spoken of as illumination.

SANS ENTHUSIASTIC

I don't know
what it is that I must ask,
you be better at giving
I cannot have your closeness upon the stroke of day nor snuggle, chilled at the curtain's draw
many happenings of the day
catch me unaware
I keep pouting for rain of mercy and kindness
I would gladly welcome
it is that I am sans enthusiastic
gorging always the surrealistic and getting hurtled in the wake.

ARTIFICIAL HUES

Artificial hues and the not so godly
are fostered by slime
the light of plastic to leaven
rays of God ,skelter
alas! the rude so plunder
care be upon you
all , who walk with trepidation
attain, that picturesque!
the artificial hues are in truth distracting
are similies of universal perfectitude.

OF GLORIA

The petals of the May- flower scatter
upon the ground rich to tread
the earth's treasure askew bequeathed
and there lo! , goes the women
vain about their gowns of varying shades
borrowed from the mother
glad in their hearts at the artiste of loom
about which is made of amuch
the burden that love bears does never collapse
the loitering never cease
the pranks and prances of folks,
men and women ever recast into relations of gloria.

BETWIXT THE TWIGS

Flicker that a lamp shed
wiping the heat breathless
walking away from ruin
it could get cold,
colder
something that intones,
voices repeatedly felt
must be the conscience
which loves to be soothed, indulged, comforted
and prefers , alas! not to be way-ward
but to huddle, eager, some where it finds togetherness,
the closeness, succinct betwixt twigs of the peepal.

LIBERATION

The fetters whence removed
liberation does come in the wake
redressing errors weakly done
harsh repertoire of the past then to be pardoned infatuation forgiven
the cosmos is the sport of God, wherein the world is a stage where a drama is enacted
at the end of the enrollment the characters withdraw the curtain being drawn
there be nor day nor night
the azurre heavens bidding
speaking not of merit nor sin
the ambre sky, surely caution
of better and better a time
ceaseless enjoyment be begotten.